THIRD EDITION

PIANO • VOCAL • GUITAR

125 OF BROADWAY'S BEST LOVED MELODIES

Broadway Deluxe

Broadway, with all its glitter and glamour, has been entertaining millions of show-goers for decades. And the Broadway musical has always been an outstanding source of memorable songs.

This songbook contains an exciting collection of 125 of Broadway's best! We invite you to enjoy what is one of the most extraordinary song-books of its kind ever published.

ISBN 0-88188-306-9

HAL•LEONARD®
CORPORATION
7777 W. BLUEMOUND RD. P.O. BOX 13819 MILWAUKEE, WI 53213

Visit Hal Leonard Online at
www.halleonard.com

SONG INDEX

Handwritten note next to 266 "Till There Was You": "Audition ... 8, 16, +32"

SHOW INDEX

ELABORATE LIVES

from Walt Disney Theatrical Productions' AIDA

Music by ELTON JOHN
Lyrics by TIM RICE

true _____

This may not be the mo-ment

to tell you face to face

But I could wait for -

ev-er _____

for the per-fect time _____ and place _____

rall.

RADAMES:

AIDA: We all lead

such e-lab-o-rate lives _____

WRITTEN IN THE STARS

from Walt Disney Teatrical Productions' AIDA

Music by ELTON JOHN
Lyrics by TIM RICE

AIN'T MISBEHAVIN'
from AIN'T MISBEHAVIN'

Words by ANDY RAZAF
Music by THOMAS "FATS" WALLER and HARRY BROOKS

JOHNNY ONE NOTE

from BABES IN ARMS

Words by LORENZ HART
Music by RICHARD RODGERS

WHERE OR WHEN
from BABES IN ARMS

Words by LORENZ HART
Music by RICHARD RODGERS

THE LADY IS A TRAMP

from BABES IN ARMS

Words by LORENZ HART
Music by RICHARD RODGERS

MY FUNNY VALENTINE

from BABES IN ARMS

Words by LORENZ HART
Music by RICHARD RODGERS

JUST IN TIME
from BELLS ARE RINGING

Words by BETTY COMDEN
and ADOLPH GREEN
Music by JULE STYNE

THE PARTY'S OVER

from BELLS ARE RINGING

Words by BETTY COMDEN
and ADOLPH GREEN
Music by JULE STYNE

THIS CAN'T BE LOVE

from THE BOYS FROM SYRACUSE

Words by LORENZ HART
Music by RICHARD RODGERS

My heart does not stand still,_____ Just hear it beat! This is too sweet to be love. This can't be love be-cause I feel so well;_____ But still I love to look_____ in your eyes._____ eyes.

FALLING IN LOVE WITH LOVE

from THE BOYS FROM SYRACUSE

Words by LORENZ HART
Music by RICHARD RODGERS

Moderate Waltz

CABARET
from the Musical CABARET

Words by FRED EBB
Music by JOHN KANDER

What good is sit-ting a-lone in your room?
Put down the knit-ting, the book and the broom,

Come hear the mu-sic play;
Time for a hol-i-day;

Life is a cab-a-ret, old chum, Come to the

cab - a - ret. _____ ret. Come taste the

wine, Come hear the band, Come blow the horn, start

cel - e - brat - ing, Right this way, your ta - ble's wait - ing. No use per -
Start by ad -

mit - ting some proph - et of doom _ To wipe ev - 'ry smile a -
mit - ting from cra - dle to tomb _____ is - n't that long a

WILLKOMMEN
from the Musical CABARET

Words by FRED EBB
Music by JOHN KANDER

With spirit

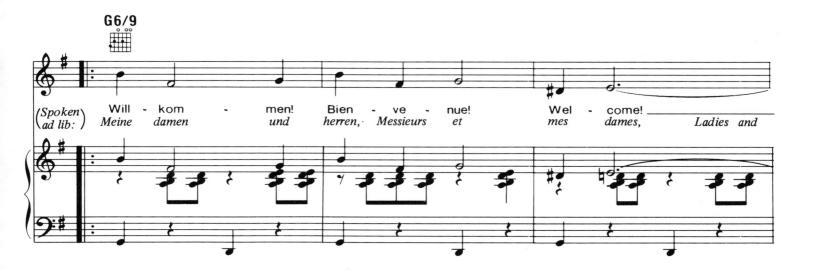

(Spoken ad lib:) Will - kom - men! Bien - ve - nue! Wel - come! _____
Meine damen und herren, Messieurs et mes dames, Ladies and

_____ gentlemen,
Frem - der,
Guten abend,

E - tran - ger,
Bon soir,

CAMELOT
from CAMELOT

Words by ALAN JAY LERNER
Music by FREDERICK LOEWE

I LOVED YOU ONCE IN SILENCE
from CAMELOT

Words by ALAN JAY LERNER
Music by FREDERICK LOEWE

Moderately

IF EVER I WOULD LEAVE YOU

from CAMELOT

Words by ALAN JAY LERNER
Music by FREDERICK LOEWE

I LOVE PARIS

from CAN-CAN

Words and Music by
COLE PORTER

Ev - 'ry time I look down on this time - less town, wheth - er blue or gray be her skies, wheth - er loud be her

I love Par - is in the win - ter when it driz - zles,

I love Par - is in the sum - mer when it siz - zles.

I love Par - is ev - 'ry mo - ment,_____

ev - 'ry mo - ment of the year._____

IT'S ALL RIGHT WITH ME

from CAN-CAN

Words and Music by
COLE PORTER

Steadily moving fox trot

It's the wrong time _____ and the wrong place _____ tho' your face is charm-

-ing it's the wrong face, _____ it's not {her}{his} face _____ but such a charm - ing face _____

that It's All Right _____ With Me. _____ It's the wrong song _____

MEMORY
from CATS

Music by ANDREW LLOYD WEBBER
Text by TREVOR NUNN after T.S. ELIOT

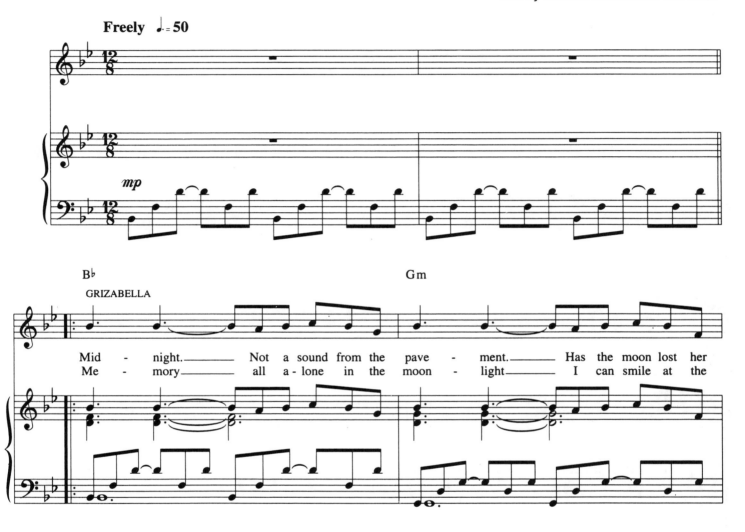

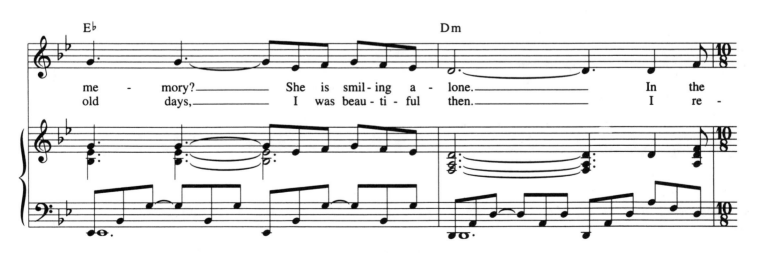

GRIZABELLA

Mid - night._____ Not a sound from the pave - ment._____ Has the moon lost her
Me - mory_____ all a - lone in the moon - light_____ I can smile at the

me - mory?_____ She is smil-ing a - lone._____ In the
old days,_____ I was beau-ti-ful then._____ I re -

a tempo

Day - light.___ I must wait for the sun - rise,___ I must think of a new life___ and I must - n't give

in._____ When the dawn comes to - night will be a me - mo - ry too___ and a

new day_____ will be - gin.

AND ALL THAT JAZZ
from CHICAGO

Words by FRED EBB
Music by JOHN KANDER

TRY TO REMEMBER

from THE FANTASTICKS

Words by TOM JONES
Music by HARVEY SCHMIDT

Slowly, with tenderness

HOW ARE THINGS IN GLOCCA MORRA

from FINIAN'S RAINBOW

Words by E.Y. HARBURG
Music by BURTON LANE

IF THIS ISN'T LOVE
from FINIAN'S RAINBOW

Words by E.Y. HARBURG
Music by BURTON LANE

LOOK TO THE RAINBOW

from FINIAN'S RAINBOW

Words by E.Y. HARBURG
Music by BURTON LANE

OLD DEVIL MOON

from FINIAN'S RAINBOW

Words by E.Y. HARBURG
Music by BURTON LANE

MAKE SOMEONE HAPPY

from DO RE MI

Words by BETTY COMDEN
and ADOLPH GREEN
Music by JULE STYNE

LOVE, LOOK AWAY

from FLOWER DRUM SONG

Lyrics by OSCAR HAMMERSTEIN II
Music by RICHARD RODGERS

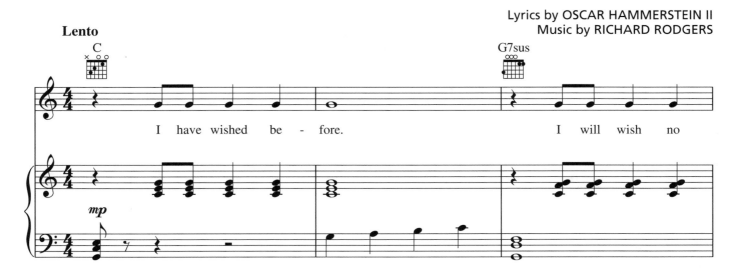

I have wished be - fore. I will wish no

more. Love, look a - way! Love, look a - way from

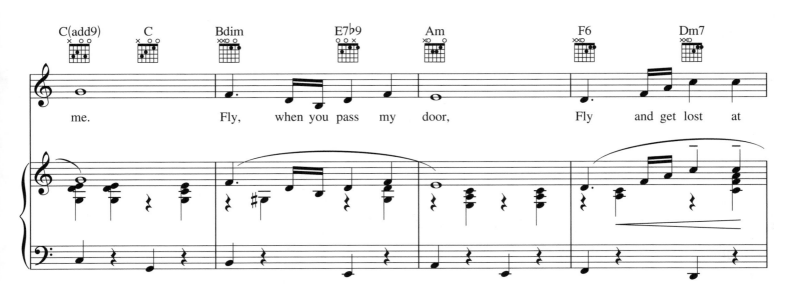

me. Fly, when you pass my door, Fly and get lost at

I ENJOY BEING A GIRL

from FLOWER DRUM SONG

Lyrics by OSCAR HAMMERSTEIN II
Music by RICHARD RODGERS

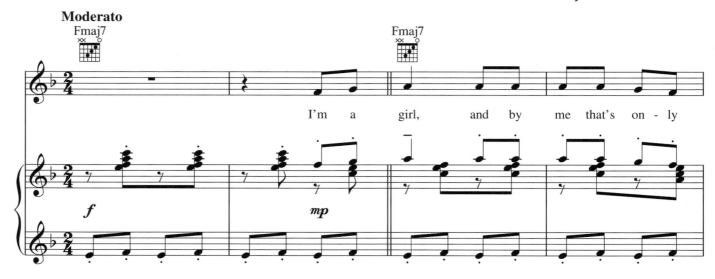

Refrain *(brightly)*

BUTTON UP YOUR OVERCOAT

from FOLLOW THRU

Words and Music by B.G. DeSYLVA,
LEW BROWN and RAY HENDERSON

YOU RULE MY WORLD

from THE FULL MONTY

Words and Music by
DAVID YAZBEK

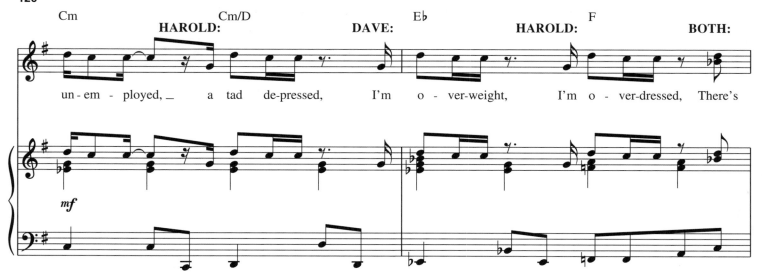

HAROLD: **DAVE:** **HAROLD:** **BOTH:**

un-em-ployed, _ a tad de-pressed, I'm o-ver-weight, I'm o-ver-dressed, There's

DAVE:

noth-ing I _ can do, _ you rule _ my _ world. _ There's

Slower

noth-ing I _ can do... _

DON'T RAIN ON MY PARADE

from FUNNY GIRL

Words by BOB MERRILL
Music by JULE STYNE

PEOPLE
from FUNNY GIRL

Words by BOB MERRILL
Music by JULE STYNE

need - ing oth - er chil - dren, _____ and yet,

Bbm C7 Fmaj7 F6 G Bbm6 Bbdim7

let - ting our grown - up pride Hide all the need in -

F/A Abdim7 Gm7 C7

side, act - ing more like chil - dren than

E/F F7 Cm7 F9 Bb

chil - dren. _____ Lov - ers _____

rit. *a tempo*

COMEDY TONIGHT
from A FUNNY THING HAPPENED ON THE WAY TO THE FORUM

Words and Music by
STEPHEN SONDHEIM

Some - thing fa - mil - iar, some - thing pe - cul - iar,
Some - thing con - vul - sive, some - thing re - pul - sive,

Some - thing for ev - 'ry - one, a com - e - dy to - night!
Some - thing for ev - 'ry - one, a com - e - dy to - night!

Some - thing ap - peal - ing some - thing ap - pal - ling,
Some - thing es - thet - ic, some - thing fre - net - ic,

LIFE IS JUST A BOWL OF CHERRIES

from GEORGE WHITE'S SCANDALS (1931 Edition)

Words and Music by LEW BROWN
and RAY HENDERSON

I REMEMBER IT WELL

from GIGI

Words by ALAN JAY LERNER
Music by FREDERICK LOEWE

DAY BY DAY

from the Musical GODSPELL

Words and Music by
STEPHEN SCHWARTZ

THE BEST THINGS IN LIFE ARE FREE

from GOOD NEWS!

Music and Lyrics by B. G. DeSYLVA,
LEW BROWN and RAY HENDERSON

A BUSHEL AND A PECK

from GUYS AND DOLLS

By FRANK LOESSER

IF I WERE A BELL
from GUYS AND DOLLS

Medium Bounce

By FRANK LOESSER

Ask me how do I feel___ Ask me now that we're co-sy and cling - ing___
how do I feel___ From this Chem-is-try les-son I'm learn - ing___

Well sir, all I can say___ is if I ___ were a bell___ I'd be
Well sir, all I can say___ is if I ___ were a bridge___ I'd be

ring - ing.___ From the mo-ment we kissed to-nite___
burn - ing.___ Yes, I knew my mor - ale would crack___

EVERYTHING'S COMING UP ROSES

from GYPSY

Words by STEPHEN SONDHEIM
Music by JULE STYNE

LET ME ENTERTAIN YOU

from GYPSY

Words by STEPHEN SONDHEIM
Music by JULE STYNE

Moderately

So let me en-ter-tain you, let me make you smile. Let me do a few tricks, some old and then some new tricks; I'm ver-y ver-sa-tile.

SMALL WORLD

from GYPSY

Words by STEPHEN SONDHEIM
Music by JULE STYNE

TOGETHER WHEREVER WE GO

from GYPSY

Words by STEPHEN SONDHEIM
Music by JULE STYNE

I CAN HEAR THE BELLS

from HAIRSPRAY

Music by MARC SHAIMAN
Lyrics by MARC SHAIMAN and SCOTT WITTMAN

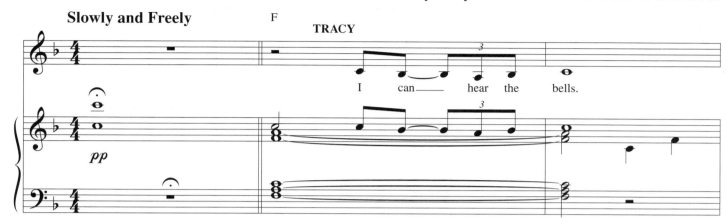

Slowly and Freely

TRACY

I can ___ hear the bells.

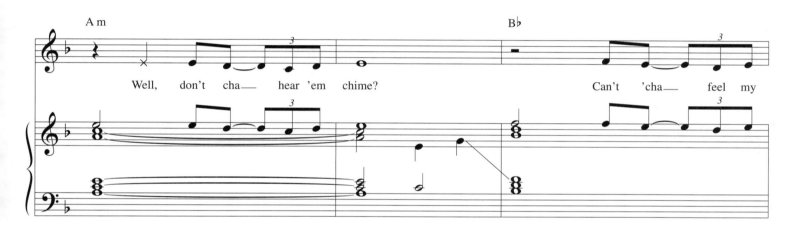

Well, don't cha ___ hear 'em chime?

Can't 'cha ___ feel my

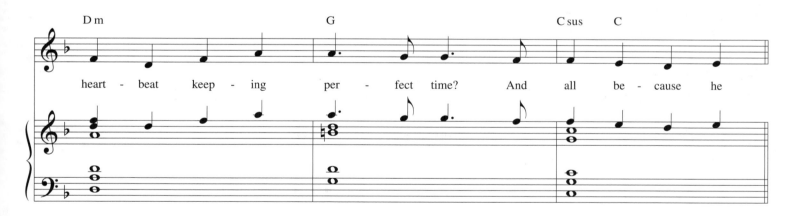

heart - beat keep - ing per - fect time? And all be - cause he

Moderate Rock Beat

touched me. He looked at ___ me and stared. Yes, he bumped me. My

IT TAKES TWO
from HAIRSPRAY

Music by MARC SHAIMAN
Lyrics by MARC SHAIMAN and SCOTT WITTMAN

They say it's a man's world. Well, that can-not be de-nied.
A king ain't a king with-out the pow'r be-hind the throne.
Just like Frank-ie Av-a-lon has his fav-'rite Mouse-ke-teer,

But what good's a man's world with-out a wom-an by his side?
A prince is a pau-per, babe, with-out a chick to call his own.
I dream of a lov-er, babe, to say the things I long to hear.

RUN AND TELL THAT

from HAIRSPRAY

Music by MARC SHAIMAN
Lyrics by MARC SHAIMAN and SCOTT WITTMAN

LI'L INEZ, SEAWEED & ENSEMBLE

deep as a riv - er and soars to the sky!

SEAWEED

I can't see the rea-son it can't be the kind-a world where we all get our chance.

The time is now, and we can show them how to turn the

BEFORE THE PARADE PASSES BY

from HELLO, DOLLY!

Music and Lyric by
JERRY HERMAN

MY CUP RUNNETH OVER

from I DO! I DO!

Words by TOM JONES
Music by HARVEY SCHMIDT

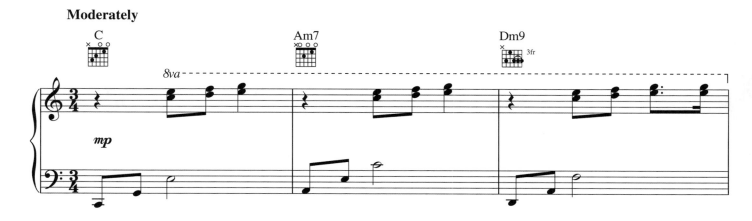

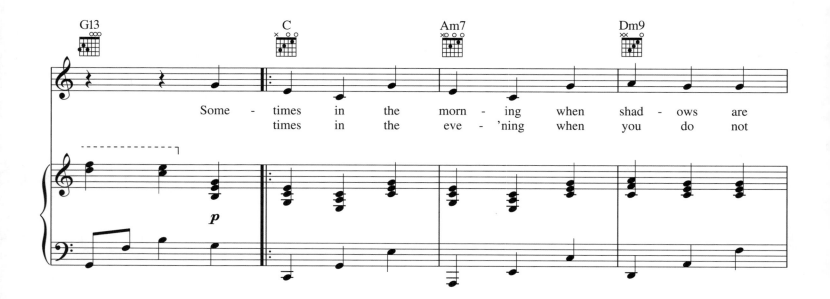

Some - times in the morn - ing when shad - ows are
times in the eve - 'ning when when you do not

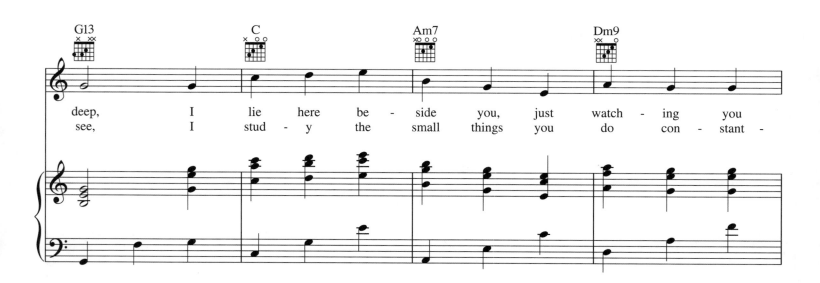

deep, I lie here be - side you, just watch - ing you
see, I stud - y the small things you do con - stant -

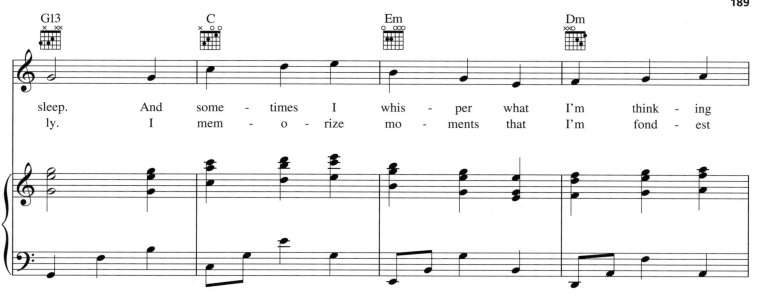

sleep.   And   some - times   I   whis - per what I'm think - ing
ly.   I   mem - o - rize mo - ments that I'm fond - est

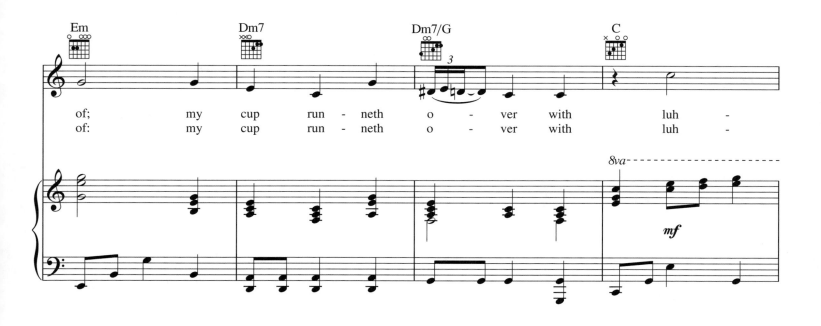

of;   my cup run - neth o - ver with   luh -
of: my cup run - neth o - ver with   luh

uh - uh - uh - uh -
uh - uh - uh - uh -

SOMEONE LIKE YOU

from JEKYLL & HYDE

Words by LESLIE BRICUSSE
Music by FRANK WILDHORN

Slowly, with expression

I peered through win-dows, watched life go by. Dreamed of to-mor-row,
It's like you took my dreams, made each one real. You reached in-side of me

but stayed in-side. The past was hold-ing me,
and made me feel. And now I see a world

AND THIS IS MY BELOVED

from KISMET

Words and Music by ROBERT WRIGHT and GEORGE FORREST
(Music Based on Themes of A. BORODIN)

STRANGER IN PARADISE

from KISMET

Words and Music by ROBERT WRIGHT
and GEORGE FORREST
(Music Based on Themes of A. BORODIN)

I WHISTLE A HAPPY TUNE

from THE KING AND I

Lyrics by OSCAR HAMMERSTEIN II
Music by RICHARD RODGERS

hap - pi - ness in the tune con - vinc - es me that

I'm not a - fraid.

Coda

Make be - lieve you're brave And the trick will take you far.

You may be as brave as you make be - lieve you

GETTING TO KNOW YOU

from THE KING AND I

Lyrics by OSCAR HAMMERSTEIN II
Music by RICHARD RODGERS

HELLO, YOUNG LOVERS

from THE KING AND I

Lyrics by OSCAR HAMMERSTEIN II
Music by RICHARD RODGERS

Refrain *(very moderately)*

lo, young lov-ers, who-ev-er you are, I hope your trou-bles are few _____ All my good wish-es go with you to-night— I've been in love like you. _____ Be brave, young lov-ers, and fol-low your

I HAVE DREAMED
from THE KING AND I

Lyrics by OSCAR HAMMERSTEIN II
Music by RICHARD RODGERS

WE KISS IN A SHADOW

from THE KING AND I

Lyrics by OSCAR HAMMERSTEIN II
Music by RICHARD RODGERS

sigh   For one smil-ing day to be

free _____ To kiss in the

sun-light   And say to the sky _____

Be-hold and be-lieve what you see! _____

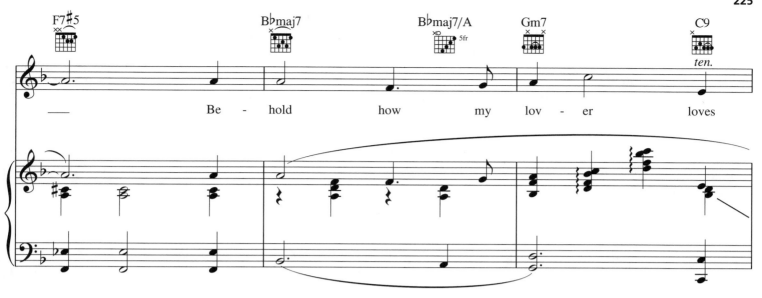

Be - hold how my lov - er loves

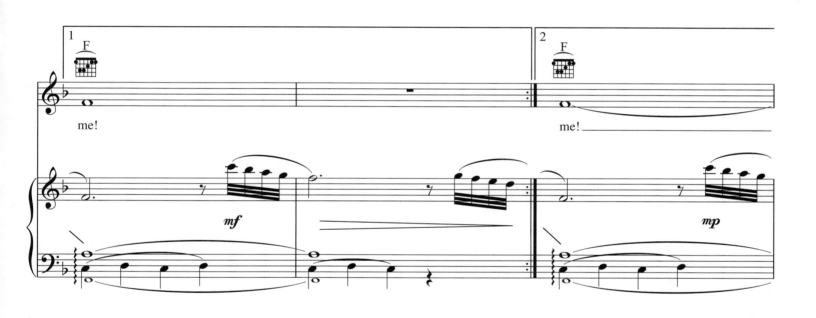

me!

me!

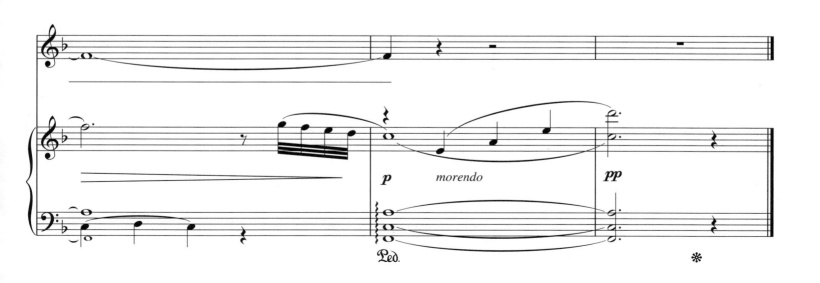

SEPTEMBER SONG
from the Musical Play KNICKERBOCKER HOLIDAY

Words by MAXWELL ANDERSON
Music by KURT WEILL

MY HEART BELONGS TO DADDY

from LEAVE IT TO ME

Words and Music by
COLE PORTER

ANOTHER OP'NIN', ANOTHER SHOW

from KISS ME, KATE

Words and Music by
COLE PORTER

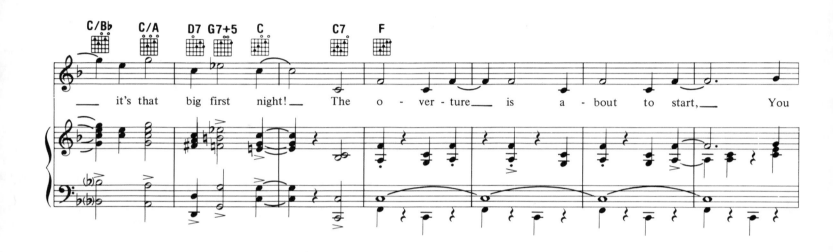

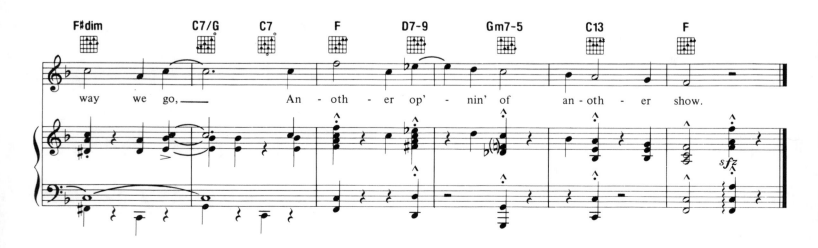

CASTLE ON A CLOUD
from LES MISÉRABLES

Music by CLAUDE-MICHEL SCHÖNBERG
Lyrics by ALAIN BOUBLIL, JEAN-MARC NATEL
and HERBERT KRETZMER

BRING HIM HOME
from LES MISÉRABLES

Music by CLAUDE-MICHEL SCHÖNBERG
Lyrics by ALAIN BOUBLIL and HERBERT KRETZMER

SHADOWLAND
Disney Presents THE LION KING: THE BROADWAY MUSICAL

Music by LEBO M and HANS ZIMMER
Lyrics by MARK MANCINA and LEBO M

MR. WONDERFUL

from the Musical MR. WONDERFUL

Words and Music by JERRY BOCK,
LARRY HOLOFCENER and GEORGE DAVID WEISS

Slowly and expressively

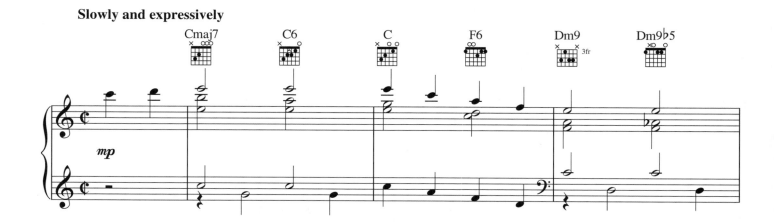

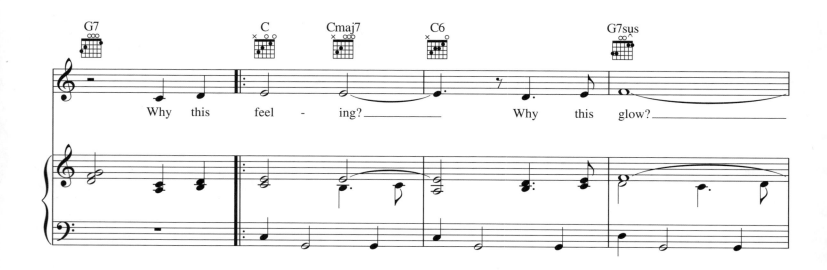

Why this feel - ing? _____ Why this glow? _____

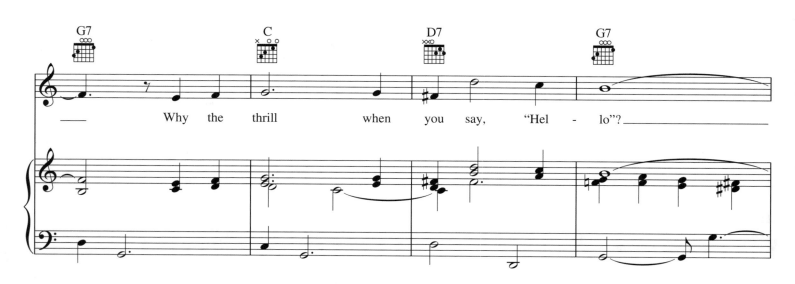

_____ Why the thrill when you say, "Hel - lo"? _____

STANDING ON THE CORNER

from THE MOST HAPPY FELLA

By FRANK LOESSER

HERMAN and BOYS:

Stand - ing on the cor - ner watch - ing all the girls go by,
Stand - ing on the cor - ner watch - ing all the girls go by,
Stand - ing on the cor - ner watch - ing all the girls go by,

Stand - ing on the cor - ner watch - ing all the girls go
Stand - ing on the cor - ner giv - ing all the girls the
Stand - ing on the cor - ner un - der-neath a spring - time

by
eye
sky

Broth-er you don't know a nic - er oc - cu -
Broth-er if you've got a rich i - mag - i -
Broth-er you can't go to jail for what you're

SEVENTY SIX TROMBONES

from Meredith Willson's THE MUSIC MAN

By MEREDITH WILLSON

took my place as the one and on - ly bass, and I oom - pahed,

oom - pahed, oom - pah - pahed, oom - pahed up and down the

square. Sev - en - ty square.

TILL THERE WAS YOU
from Meredith Willson's THE MUSIC MAN

By MEREDITH WILLSON

There were bells on the hill, but I never heard them ringing. No, I

nev-er heard them at all 'till there was you._____ There were

birds in the sky, but I never saw them winging, No, I

GET ME TO THE CHURCH ON TIME

from MY FAIR LADY

Words by ALAN JAY LERNER
Music by FREDERICK LOEWE

I COULD HAVE DANCED ALL NIGHT

from MY FAIR LADY

Words by ALAN JAY LERNER
Music by FREDERICK LOEWE

Brightly

I Could Have Danced _____ All Night! _____ I Could Have
Danced _____ All Night! _____ And still _____
_____ have begged _____ for more. _____

I could have spread _____ my wings _____

And done a thou - sand things _____ I've

nev - er done _____ be - fore _____

I'll nev - er know _____ what made it so _____ ex -

cit - ing, _____ Why all at once _____ my

I'VE GROWN ACCUSTOMED TO HER FACE

from MY FAIR LADY

Words by ALAN JAY LERNER
Music by FREDERICK LOEWE

ON THE STREET WHERE YOU LIVE

from MY FAIR LADY

Words by ALAN JAY LERNER
Music by FREDERICK LOEWE

THE RAIN IN SPAIN

from MY FAIR LADY

Words by ALAN JAY LERNER
Music by FREDERICK LOEWE

SHOW ME
from MY FAIR LADY

Words by ALAN JAY LERNER
Music by FREDERICK LOEWE

Don't talk to stars burn - ing a - bove.

If you're in love, show me!

Tell me no dreams filled with de - sire.

WOULDN'T IT BE LOVERLY

from MY FAIR LADY

Words by ALAN JAY LERNER
Music by FREDERICK LOEWE

WITH A LITTLE BIT OF LUCK

from MY FAIR LADY

Words by ALAN JAY LERNER
Music by FREDERICK LOEWE

THE SWEETEST SOUNDS

from NO STRINGS

Lyrics and Music by
RICHARD RODGERS

OKLAHOMA
from OKLAHOMA!

Lyrics by OSCAR HAMMERSTEIN II
Music by RICHARD RODGERS

OH, WHAT A BEAUTIFUL MORNIN'

from OKLAHOMA!

Lyrics by OSCAR HAMMERSTEIN II
Music by RICHARD RODGERS

PEOPLE WILL SAY WE'RE IN LOVE

from OKLAHOMA!

Lyrics by OSCAR HAMMERSTEIN II
Music by RICHARD RODGERS

rose and my glove.
fade from a - bove.

Sweet - heart they're sus - pect - ing things.
They'll see it's al - right with me.

Peo - ple will say we're in love.
Peo - ple will say we're in

love.

THE SURREY WITH THE FRINGE ON TOP

from OKLAHOMA!

Lyrics by OSCAR HAMMERSTEIN II
Music by RICHARD RODGERS

Refrain

Chicks and ducks and geese bet - ter scur - ry when I take you
All the world - 'll fly in a flur - ry when I take you
I can see the stars get - tin' blur - ry when we drive back

out in the sur - rey, when I take you out in the sur - rey with the
out in the sur - rey, when I take you out in the sur - rey with the
home in the sur - rey, driv - in' slow - ly home in the sur - rey with the

rig, I'm a - think - in' you c'n keep your rig if you're think - in' 'at I'd
go on for - ev - er? Don't you wisht y'd go on for - ev - er and ud
dream worth a - keep - in', whoa! you team, and jist keep a - creep - in' at a

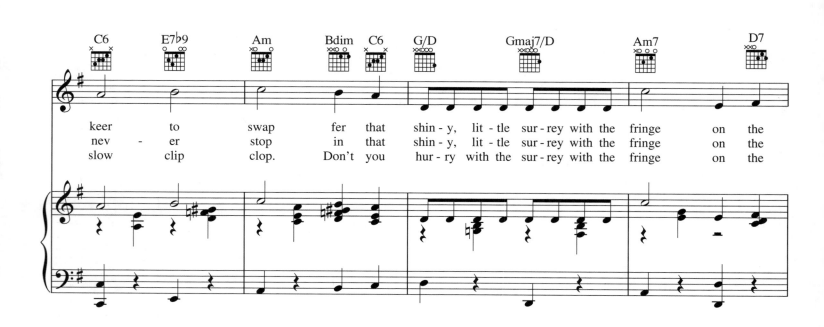

keer to swap fer that shin - y, lit - tle sur - rey with the fringe on the
nev - er stop in that shin - y, lit - tle sur - rey with the fringe on the
slow clip clop. Don't you hur - ry with the sur - rey with the fringe on the

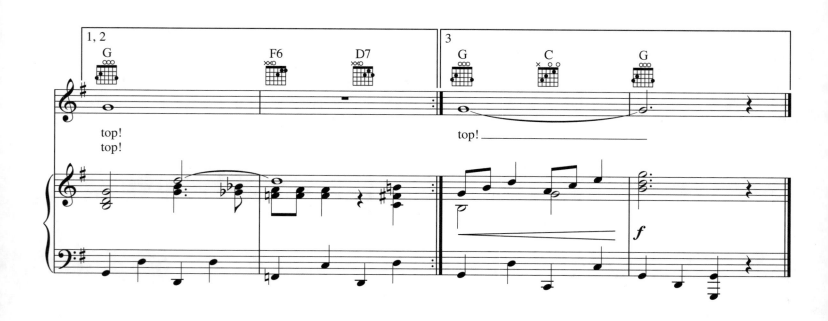

top!
top!

top!

CONSIDER YOURSELF

from the Columbia Pictures - Romulus Motion Picture Production of Lionel Bart's OLIVER!

Words and Music by
LIONEL BART

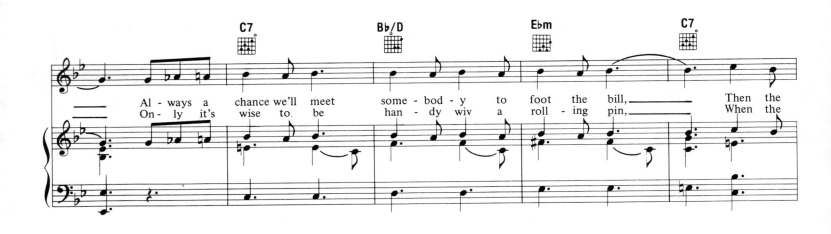

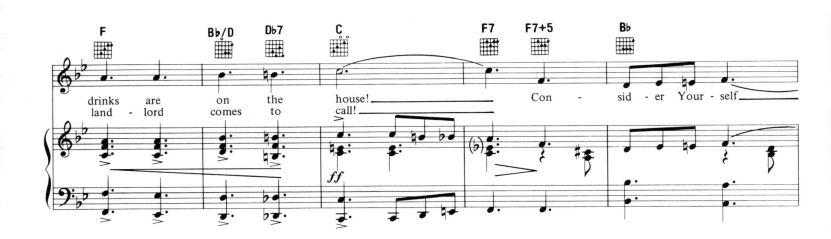

AS LONG AS HE NEEDS ME

from the Columbia Pictures - Romulus Motion Picture Production of Lionel Bart's OLIVER!

Words and Music by
LIONEL BART

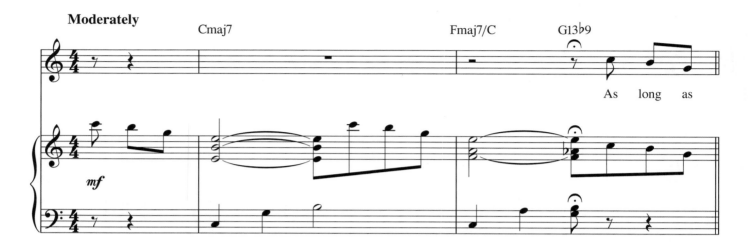

ON A CLEAR DAY
(You Can See Forever)
from ON A CLEAR DAY YOU CAN SEE FOREVER

Words by ALAN JAY LERNER
Music by BURTON LANE

WHAT DID I HAVE THAT I DON'T HAVE?

from ON A CLEAR DAY YOU CAN SEE FOREVER

Words by ALAN JAY LERNER
Music by BURTON LANE

Slowly with expression

THERE'S A SMALL HOTEL

from ON YOUR TOES

Words by LORENZ HART
Music by RICHARD RODGERS

There's a small ho-tel With a wish-ing well; I wish that we were there to-geth - er. There's a brid-al suite; One room bright and neat, Com -

SPEAK LOW

from the Musical Production ONE TOUCH OF VENUS

Words by OGDEN NASH
Music by KURT WEILL

FROM THIS MOMENT ON

from OUT OF THIS WORLD

Words and Music by
COLE PORTER

I TALK TO THE TREES

from PAINT YOUR WAGON

Words by ALAN JAY LERNER
Music by FREDERICK LOEWE

THEY CALL THE WIND MARIA

from PAINT YOUR WAGON

Words by ALAN JAY LERNER
Music by FREDERICK LOEWE

BEWITCHED

from PAL JOEY

Words by LORENZ HART
Music by RICHARD RODGERS

He's a fool and don't I know it. But a fool can have his charms.
Love's the same old sad sen - sa - tion. Late - ly I've not slept a wink.

I'm in love and don't I show it, like a babe in arms.
Since this half - pint im - i - ta - tion

put me on the blink. I'm wild a - gain, be - guiled a - gain, a

I COULD WRITE A BOOK

from PAL JOEY

Words by LORENZ HART
Music by RICHARD RODGERS

THE MUSIC OF THE NIGHT
from THE PHANTOM OF THE OPERA

Music by ANDREW LLOYD WEBBER
Lyrics by CHARLES HART
Additional Lyrics by RICHARD STILGOE

thoughts of the life you knew be - fore! Close your eyes let your spi - rit start to

soar and you'll live as you've nev - er lived be - fore.

Soft - ly, deft - ly, mu - sic shall ca - ress you. Hear it, feel it,

se - cret - ly pos - sess you. O - pen up your mind let your fan - ta - sies un - wind in this

Float - ing, fall - ing, sweet in - tox - i - ca - tion. Touch me, trust me,

sa - vour each sen - sa - tion. Let the dream be - gin, let your dark - er side give in to the

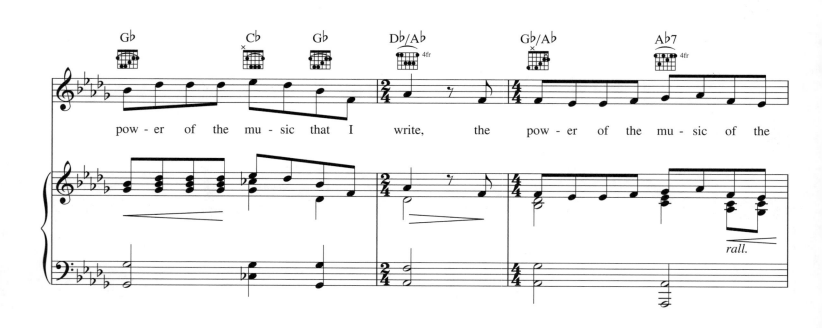

pow - er of the mu - sic that I write, the pow - er of the mu - sic of the

IF I RULED THE WORLD

from PICKWICK

Words by LESLIE BRICUSSE
Music by CYRIL ORNADEL

'TIL HIM
from THE PRODUCERS

Music and Lyrics by
MEL BROOKS

Moderate Ballad

LEO: No one ev - er made me feel like some - one 'til him.

Life was real - ly noth - ing but a glum one 'til him.

My ex - ist - ence bor - dered on the trag - ic, al - ways tim - id, nev - er took a

THAT FACE

from THE PRODUCERS

Music and Lyrics by
MEL BROOKS

Slowly and Sweetly

LEO: **Freely, moving forward**

The urge to merge can rob us of our sens- es. The

need to breed can make a man a drone. We must be on a- lert with our de-

WHEN YOU GOT IT, FLAUNT IT

from THE PRODUCERS

Music and Lyrics by
MEL BROOKS

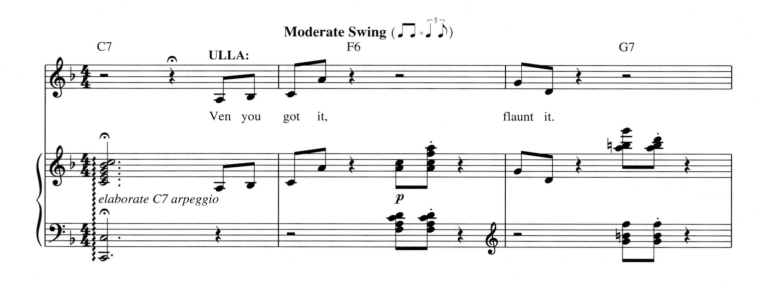

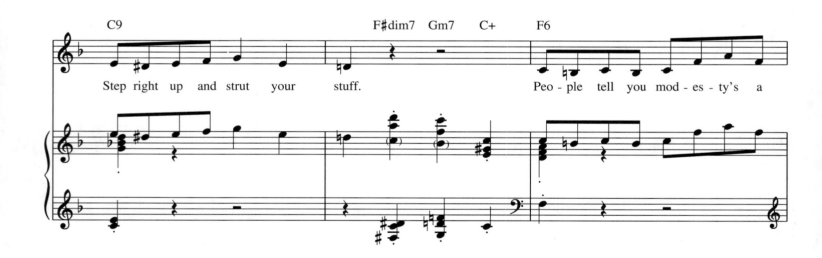

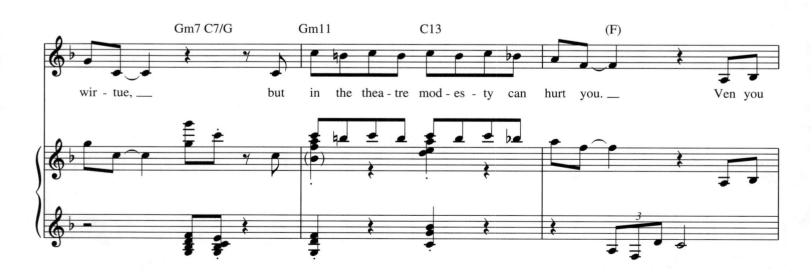

SEASONS OF LOVE

from RENT

Words and Music by
JONATHAN LARSON

ONE SONG GLORY

from RENT

Words and Music by
JONATHAN LARSON

IT'S DE-LOVELY

from RED, HOT AND BLUE!

Words and Music by
COLE PORTER

*Pronounced "delukes"

WHO CAN I TURN TO
(When Nobody Needs Me)
from THE ROAR OF THE GREASEPAINT—THE SMELL OF THE CROWD

Words and Music by LESLIE BRICUSSE
and ANTHONY NEWLEY

Slowly with expression

Who can I turn to _____ when no-bod-y needs me? _____

My heart wants to know and so I must go where

des - ti - ny leads me. _____ With no star to guide me,

A WONDERFUL DAY LIKE TODAY

from THE ROAR OF THE GREASEPAINT—THE SMELL OF THE CROWD

Words and Music by LESLIE BRICUSSE
and ANTHONY NEWLEY

On a won-der-ful day___ like to-day,___ I de-
won-der-ful morn-ing like this,___ When the

-fy an-y cloud___ to ap-pear in the sky.___
sun is as big___ as a yel-low bal-loon.

Dare an-y rain-drop to plop in my eye___ On a
E-ven the spar-rows are sing-ing in tune___ On a

COME RAIN OR COME SHINE

from ST. LOUIS WOMAN

Words by JOHNNY MERCER
Music by HAROLD ARLEN

TELL ME ON A SUNDAY
from SONG AND DANCE

Music by ANDREW LLOYD WEBBER
Lyrics by DON BLACK

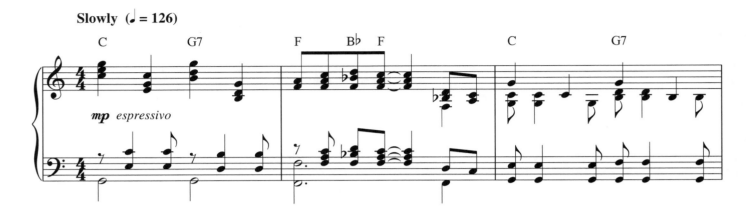

Slowly (♩ = 126)

Don't write a let-ter when you want to leave,

don't call me at 3 a. m. from a friend's a-part-ment; I'd like to choose how I

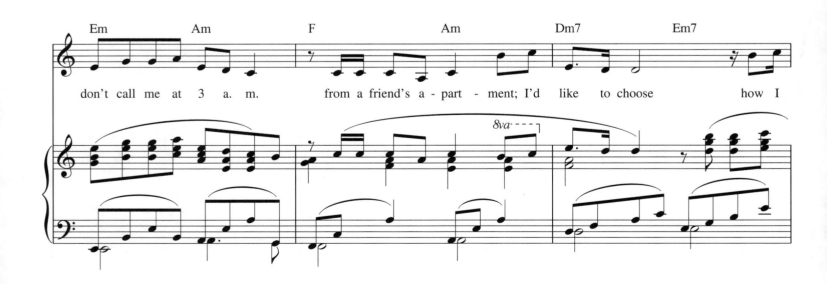

CLIMB EV'RY MOUNTAIN
from THE SOUND OF MUSIC

Lyrics by OSCAR HAMMERSTEIN II
Music by RICHARD RODGERS

Maestoso

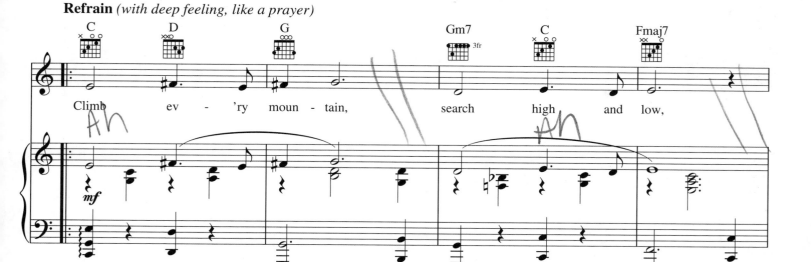

Refrain *(with deep feeling, like a prayer)*

Climb ev-'ry moun-tain, search high and low,

Fol-low ev-'ry by-way, ev-'ry path you know.

DO-RE-MI

from THE SOUND OF MUSIC

Lyrics by OSCAR HAMMERSTEIN II
Music by RICHARD RODGERS

Allegretto

GRETEL:
Let's start at the ver-y be-gin-ning!___

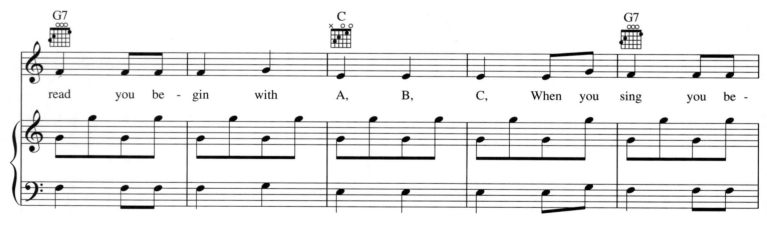

MARIA:
___ A ver-y good place to start,_____ When you

read you be-gin with A, B, C, When you sing you be-

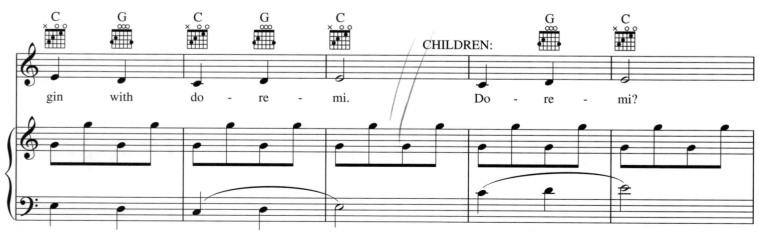

gin with do-re-mi. CHILDREN: Do-re-mi?

EDELWEISS
from THE SOUND OF MUSIC

Lyrics by OSCAR HAMMERSTEIN II
Music by RICHARD RODGERS

THE SOUND OF MUSIC
from THE SOUND OF MUSIC

Lyrics by OSCAR HAMMERSTEIN II
Music by RICHARD RODGERS

Molto moderato (*tenderly*)

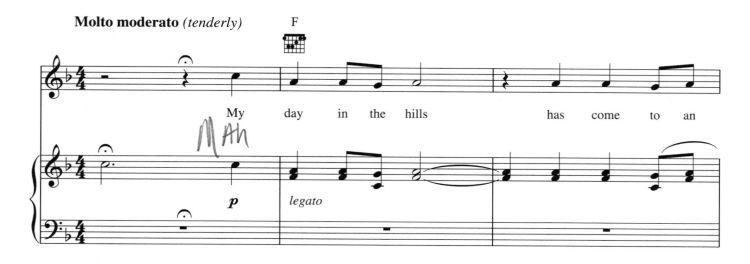

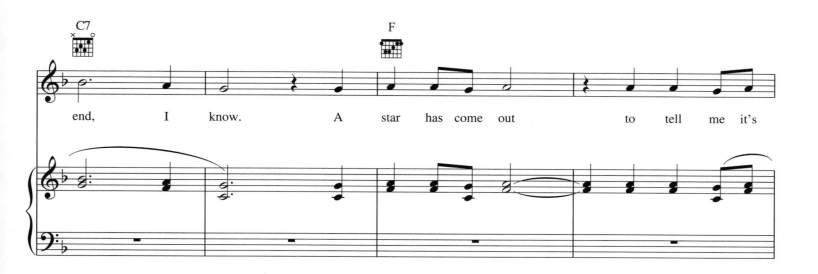

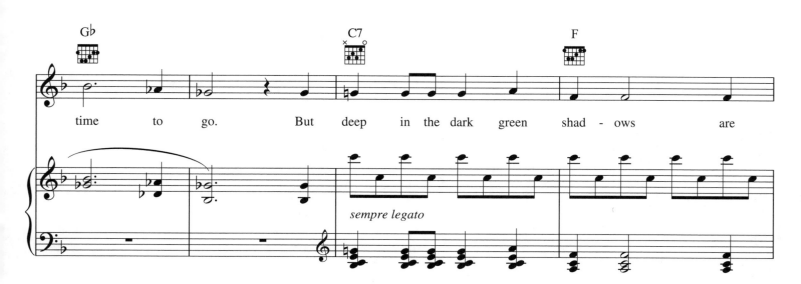

MY FAVORITE THINGS

from THE SOUND OF MUSIC

Lyrics by OSCAR HAMMERSTEIN II
Music by RICHARD RODGERS

HAPPY TALK

from SOUTH PACIFIC

Lyrics by OSCAR HAMMERSTEIN II
Music by RICHARD RODGERS

Gm/F

Float - in' in de sky,   Look - in' like a
Look - in' like a toy,   Peek - in' through de

F(add9)

lil - y on a lake;_____
branch - es of a tree;_____

Talk a - bout a bird   Learn - in' how to
Talk a - bout a girl   Talk a - bout a

Gm/F

fly   Mak - in' all de mu - sic he can
boy   Count - in' all de rip - ples on de

III Refrain

SOME ENCHANTED EVENING

from SOUTH PACIFIC

Lyrics by OSCAR HAMMERSTEIN II
Music by RICHARD RODGERS

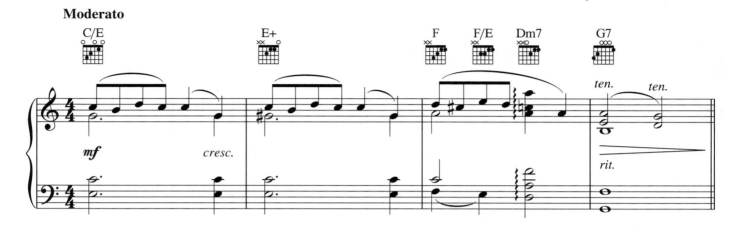

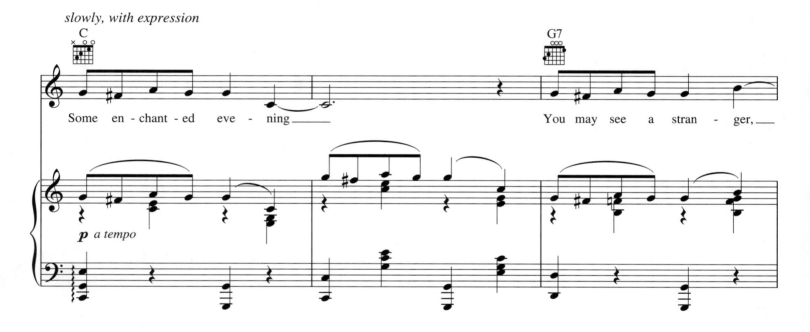

You may hear her laugh-ing _____ A - cross a crowd - ed room

And night af - ter night, _____ As strange as it seems, _____

_____ The sound of her laugh - ter will sing in your dreams. _____

Who can ex - plain it? Who can tell you why?

mf

pp *tenderly and legato*

THERE IS NOTHIN' LIKE A DAME

from SOUTH PACIFIC

Lyrics by OSCAR HAMMERSTEIN II
Music by RICHARD RODGERS

We got sun-light on the sand, We got moon-light on the sea, We got man-goes and ba-na-nas You can pick right off a tree, We got vol-ley-ball and ping-pong And a lot of dan-dy games! What ain't we got? We

THIS NEARLY WAS MINE
from SOUTH PACIFIC

Lyrics by OSCAR HAMMERSTEIN II
Music by RICHARD RODGERS

445

A WONDERFUL GUY

from SOUTH PACIFIC

Lyrics by OSCAR HAMMERSTEIN II
Music by RICHARD RODGERS

Allegro moderato

I ex-

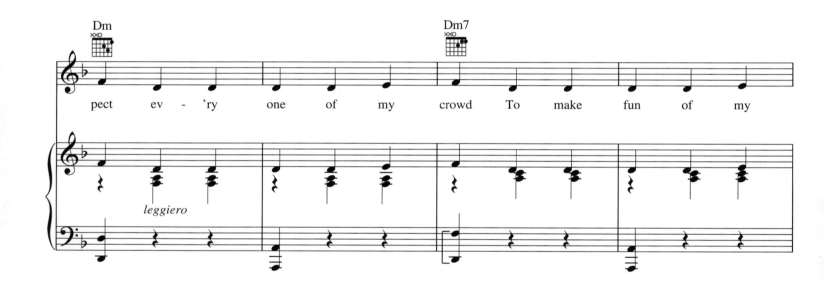

pect ev-'ry one of my crowd To make fun of my

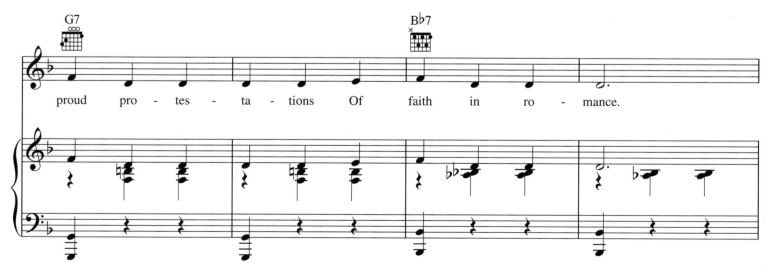

proud pro-tes-ta-tions Of faith in ro-mance.

Fear - less - ly I'll face them and ar - gue their

doubts a - way.

456

YOUNGER THAN SPRINGTIME

from SOUTH PACIFIC

Lyrics by OSCAR HAMMERSTEIN II
Music by RICHARD RODGERS

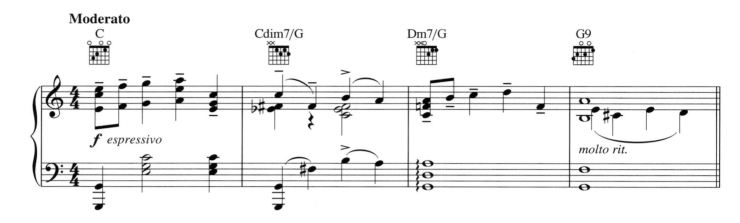

Moderato

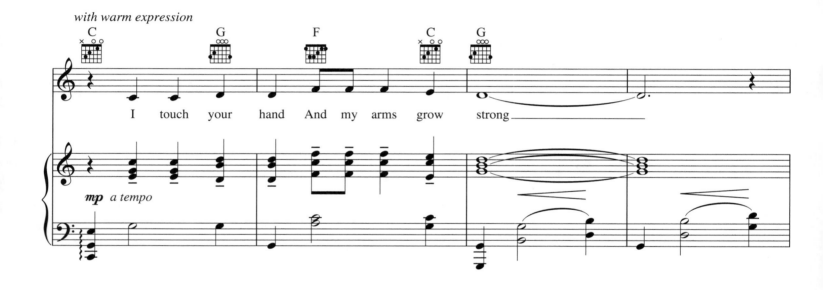

I touch your hand And my arms grow strong

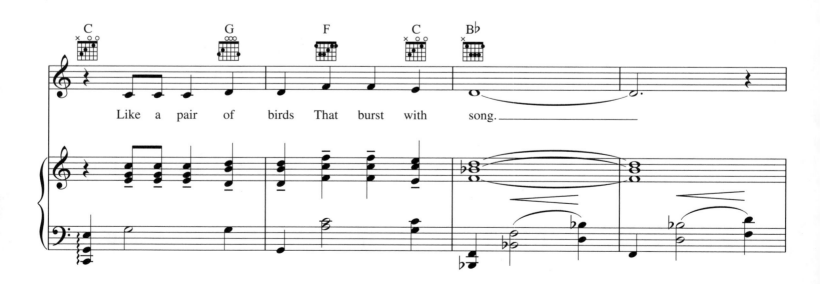

Like a pair of birds That burst with song.

IT'S A GRAND NIGHT FOR SINGING

from STATE FAIR

Lyrics by OSCAR HAMMERSTEIN II
Music by RICHARD RODGERS

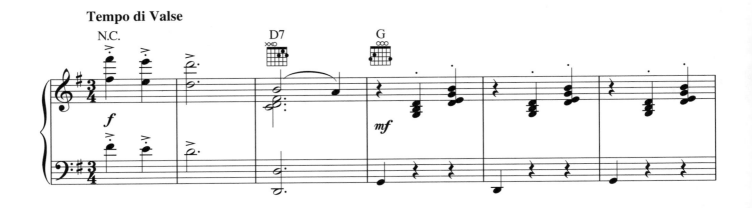

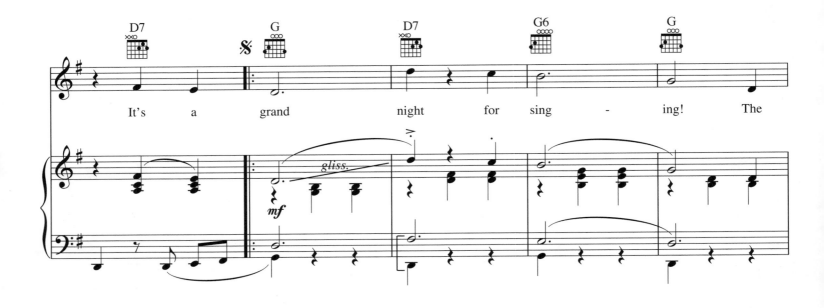

It's a grand night for sing - ing! The

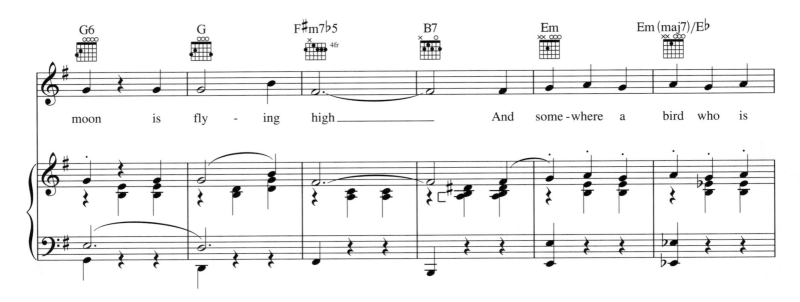

moon is fly - ing high _____ And some - where a bird who is

IT MIGHT AS WELL BE SPRING

from STATE FAIR

Lyrics by OSCAR HAMMERSTEIN II
Music by RICHARD RODGERS

AS IF WE NEVER SAID GOODBYE

from SUNSET BOULEVARD

Music by ANDREW LLOYD WEBBER
Lyrics by DON BLACK and CHRISTOPHER HAMPTON,
with contributions by AMY POWERS

GONNA BUILD A MOUNTAIN

from the Musical Production STOP THE WORLD—I WANT TO GET OFF

Words and Music by LESLIE BRICUSSE
and ANTHONY NEWLEY

Verse 3. Gon-na build a heaven from a little hell.
Gon-na build a heaven and I know darn well.
If I build my mountain with a lot of care.
And take my daydream up the mountain heaven
will be waiting there.

Verse 4. When I've built that heaven as I will some day
And the Lord sends Gabriel to take me away,
Wanna fine young son to take my place
I'll leave a son in my heav-en on earth,
With the Lord's good grace.

WHAT KIND OF FOOL AM I?

from the Musical Production STOP THE WORLD—I WANT TO GET OFF

Words and Music by LESLIE BRICUSSE
and ANTHONY NEWLEY

THEY'RE PLAYING MY SONG

from THEY'RE PLAYING OUR SONG

Words by CAROLE BAYER SAGER
Music by MARVIN HAMLISCH

8ba

ONCE IN LOVE WITH AMY

from WHERE'S CHARLEY?

By FRANK LOESSER

I AIN'T DOWN YET

from THE UNSINKABLE MOLLY BROWN

By MEREDITH WILLSON

WISH YOU WERE HERE

from WISH YOU WERE HERE

Words and Music by
HAROLD ROME

I CAN'T GET STARTED WITH YOU

from ZIEGFELD FOLLIES

Words by IRA GERSHWIN
Music by VERNON DUKE

Moderately

I'm a glum one, it's ex-plain-a-ble: I met some-one un-at-tain-a-ble.

Life's a bore, The world is my oy-ster no more.

All the pa-pers where I led the news With my ca-pers now will spread the news,